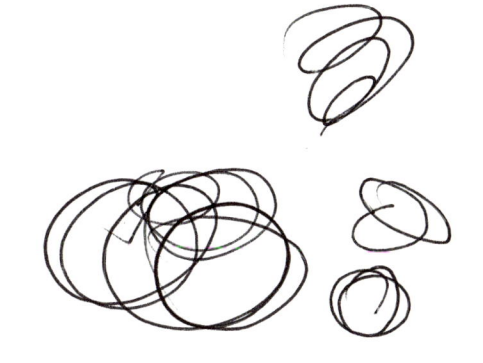

MICHAEL BARRY'S

Chocolate
THE CRAFTY WAY

JARROLD
PUBLISHING

MICHAEL BARRY'S CHOCOLATE THE CRAFTY WAY

Designed and produced by

THE ERSKINE PRESS
Banham, Norwich

for JARROLD PUBLISHING
Whitefriars, Norwich

Recipes by Michael Barry

Food photography by
The Banham Bakehouse, Norfolk

Food styling by Lesley de Boos

Photographs © Andrew Perkins

Text © Michael Barry 1998
This edition © Jarrold Publishing 1998
ISBN 0-7117-1048-1

Printed in Spain

CONTENTS

Introduction —————————— 4

Mousses ————————————— 8

Tarts and puddings ——————— 18

Cakes and baking ———————— 40

Drinks ————————————— 56

Savoury sensations ——————— 58

Index ————————————— 64

INTRODUCTION

Chocolate is the food, beyond all others, that inspires fierce passion. What other ingredient could have a dish entitled 'Death by ...', in the way that chocolate has, with the implication that this might be a pleasurable way to go? That this is so, that there are people who describe themselves as chocoholics, for whom chocolate is an addiction, is both curious and yet based in scientific fact.

Chocolate is a comparative newcomer as a food to most of the world. In fact, it's only since the middle of the nineteenth century that the worldwide obsession really began. Before then, chocolate had been merely a drink. It was a drink that at times vied with tea and coffee in popularity, but nevertheless only a drink. It had come from Mexico where, in a heavily spiced, but unsweetened form, it had been an aphrodisiac food amongst the Aztecs, reserved for the Emperor and the male members of his family. Having arrived in Europe, it was soon sweetened as a drink and widely consumed, with specialist houses, like coffee-houses but for chocolate, springing up in many capitals, including London. It wasn't until the 1820s that a Dutch *chocolatier* called Van Houten developed, in his search for lighter drinking chocolate, a way of making what we now would think of as solid eating chocolate. Chocolate had been used occasionally in baking before then and there was a well-known effect from the caffeine in chunks of ground cocoa powder mixed with sugar that were taken to help keep people awake. But, as a form of silky soft confectionery, chocolate dates from the 1840s and, in England, was produced by a firm of Quaker manufacturers called Fry.

The result of these discoveries led in the late nineteenth century and, as this book demonstrates, the twentieth, to a whole range of recipes making use of chocolate. Some of these are very simple and some spectacularly complicated, but they all depend upon the pleasure that the flavour of the cocoa bean provides. Why this pleasure should be so great has been suggested recently by a number of research projects, principally in the United States. They say that chocolate contains properties that are similar to those chemicals in the brain which produce feelings of pleasure, and also very similar in many ways to some of the biochemical mixtures known as sex hormones, particularly oestrogens, which are the principal 'female' hormones. So, it may be that when we binge on chocolate what we're really doing is cheering ourselves up and making ourselves feel sexy.

There is one last factor in the pleasure that chocolate gives, and that is its melting-point. It melts at approximately $1°$ below human body temperature, so while it goes into the mouth firm and solid, it instantaneously, but slowly, melts and coats the tongue, producing the maximum flavour impact that's possible. The combination of these things makes chocolate the most popular flavouring of sweet dishes that exists.

Chocolate can, of course, have flavours added to it. The traditional additions from Mexico were vanilla, cinnamon and chilli. While the last, to modern tastes, leaves something to be desired, vanilla and cinnamon are still wonderful partners with chocolate.

When you're buying chocolate, particularly for cooking, you need to look for dark or plain chocolate, as milk chocolate is diluted in flavour, even if it may be what you most like to eat on its own. The key factor to look for is cocoa solids. Those are the bits of the chocolate that have the maximum substance and flavour to them. The higher the level of cocoa solids that you see marked on the chocolate-bar wrapping, the better quality the flavour and therefore the chocolate itself is likely to be. It's not really worth buying anything less than 50% cocoa solids to cook with, and some of the better bars made both in Britain and on the Continent go up to 70% or above. Do check on the label, it's required now by law that the level of cocoa solids is identified.

In cooking with chocolate, unless it's going to be grated into the dish, you'll almost certainly need to melt it. There are a number of views on this, the traditional one being that it should be melted very slowly in a double boiler, that is a pan inside a pan, so that the chocolate itself never comes directly into contact with the heat, but is melted by the boiling water in the outside pan. Modern cooking often employs the use of a microwave to achieve a similar effect. The central and important point is that when you're melting chocolate you mustn't allow it to boil, because it breaks down and the texture is damaged. Then, when you mix it into the other ingredients, it doesn't blend or set so well.

Although it's not normally a recommended technique, I find that heating the chocolate in some other liquid, even a very small quantity of milk, water or orange juice, in a solid pan over a moderate heat, allows it to melt without overheating. You need to keep a careful eye on it and stir regularly, stopping the heating process as soon as the chocolate is thoroughly melted. There is also another technique, using a thick pan and moderate and direct heat, which incorporates a small piece of butter into the chocolate as it melts. You stop heating the mixture the minute the butter, which melts at a different speed from the chocolate, has completely dissolved. If it's unsalted butter and is stirred into the chocolate it will have an almost indistinguishable effect on flavour and texture. Whichever method you use, the important thing is not to overheat the chocolate, and to stir it thoroughly once it's heated to 'temper' it, which makes it much more stable in any future cooking.

Speaking of cooking, there's a wide range of chocolate dishes you'll find here – some of them very simple and some sophisticated – smooth mousses, a variety of puddings ranging from the ever-popular Italian tiramisu, through some of the more fruity French choices, to one or two English confections, which include nuts. Of course, there is a range of cakes and biscuits, including a number from America, where the development of really sticky confections halfway between cake and biscuit, known as brownies, has been developed to a fine art.

Don't forget you can also decorate things with chocolate. Proper chocolate confectioners melt the chocolate and pour it over a marble slab in a thin sheet and then either use a butter-scraper to make curls with it or cut it into elaborate shapes to make chocolate flowers or leaves. It's quite possible to make chocolate leaves in a very clever and simple way, by painting melted chocolate onto an oiled real leaf and then peeling the green leaf off later, leaving its detailed markings on the chocolate.

But really these are recipes for people who like eating chocolate as well as cooking – simple, direct and full of flavour and variation. I've added a few savoury chocolate recipes: one from its land of origin, Mexico, where it's the national tradition to cook turkey in a chocolate- and chilli-flavoured sauce, and a couple from Italy, where cooking with chocolate, for some unknown reason, appears to have reached its European peak. Whichever direction you go in, cooking with chocolate is very rewarding, and I don't just mean the nibble that the cook can have while working with it. Chocolate adds a richness and sumptuousness and a depth of flavour to both sweet and savoury dishes that few other ingredients can begin to match.

Michael Barry

CHOCOLATE MOUSSE SURPRISE

Chocolate mousse is one of the favourite puddings on every dining-table. It's extremely easy to make at home but it tends to be regarded as rather a complicated and restaurant-orientated process. Here is a recipe that includes the basic way of making chocolate mousse, but adds an unexpected additional ingredient that produces the justification for the 'surprise' in the title. It is some chopped orange peel coated in chocolate, a Belgian speciality that is now available in almost all good confectioners and chocolate shops. Mousse is, however, made with raw eggs, so I fear it is not for the elderly, the pregnant or the very young, at least if you are making it in Britain and following government advice.

INGREDIENTS
Serves 4

115 g/4 oz dark bitter chocolate, with at least 50% cocoa solids
Juice of ½ orange
25 g/1 oz butter
4 eggs
25 g/1 oz candied orange peel covered in chocolate, chopped into chunks

Melt the chocolate very carefully over a low heat in a non-stick saucepan with the orange juice. As it melts, stir it. It will go glossy and thick. When it is all completely melted, but not boiling, add the butter and stir till that has melted thoroughly too. Allow to cool slightly.

In a mixing bowl, beat the egg yolks until pale and lemon-coloured. Add to the chocolate mixture off the heat and stir carefully until well mixed. Beat the egg whites until absolutely stiff, but not grainy. Fold carefully into the chocolate – try to lose as little air as you can from the beaten egg whites.

Half-fill individual soufflé or ramekin dishes, sprinkle on the orange peel in chocolate and cover with another layer of chocolate mousse mixture. Decorate with orange peel in chocolate and chill for at least 2 hours in the fridge before serving.

MOUSSES 9

Chocolate mousse surprise

CHOCOLATE AMARETTI MOUSSE

This is a quite wonderful mousse, made with amaretti biscuits that are flavoured with apricots and almonds. As you eat the mousse you get this superb creamy, chocolatey texture and then you hit the crunchy, slightly bitter flavour of the biscuits. It is quite appallingly delicious! Contains raw eggs.

INGREDIENTS
Serves 4

175 g/6 oz dark bitter chocolate, with at least 50% cocoa solids
Juice and grated rind of 1 orange
6 eggs
55 g/2 oz unsalted butter
6 amaretti biscuits, crushed

Break the chocolate into small pieces and place it in a non-stick pan with the orange juice and rind. Then gently melt the chocolate into the orange juice, stirring occasionally until smooth and glossy. Remove from the heat.

Separate the eggs. Add the butter to the chocolate mixture, and allow it to melt in the existing heat, then stir until well blended. Add the egg yolks and stir until well combined. Whip the egg whites in a separate bowl until they are so thick you can turn the bowl upside down. Then carefully, knocking as little air out of the egg whites as possible, fold the egg whites into the chocolate mixture, using a large metal spoon. Spoon half the mousse into wine glasses, or individual bowls or into one big bowl. Sprinkle over half of the crushed amaretti biscuits and spoon on the rest of the mousse. Top with the remaining biscuits.

Place in the fridge for at least 2 hours to set.

Serve straight from the fridge.

MOUSSES 11

Chocolate amaretti mousse

CHOCOLATE MOUSSE ZAZI

For lovers of white and dark chocolate, this is the mousse for you. It is built up in layers in a tall glass. If you want to be really flashy, you can tip the glasses at an angle whilst the mousse sets, to create a zigzag of different-coloured mousse. Contains raw eggs.

INGREDIENTS
Serves 6

Juice and grated rind of 1 orange
115 g/4 oz dark bitter chocolate
Juice and grated rind of 1 lemon
115 g/4 oz white chocolate
8 eggs
55 g/2 oz unsalted butter, softened

Put the orange juice in a non-stick pan with the dark chocolate and the lemon juice into another pan with the white chocolate. Over a very mild heat melt both lots of chocolate and stir till glossy and smooth. Add the grated rind to each appropriate pan and remove from the heat.

Separate the eggs and beat 4 yolks into each of the two pans. Add the butter, dividing it between the pans, and mix thoroughly. Beat the whites until stiff, divide into two and fold half into each egg and chocolate mixture.

Take 6 tall wine glasses, put half the dark chocolate mousse into them and lay them at a 45° angle (a rolling-pin is a useful prop) in the fridge to set for 10 minutes. Remove, put half the white chocolate mousse in and lay on the opposite angle so that the chocolate forms a zigzag pattern. Repeat this using the remaining mousse. On the last filling stand the glasses upright so the top is level. If you do not have room in your fridge to try this, then fill them in alternating horizontal stripes. Decorate with grated chocolate.

MOUSSES 13

Chocolate mousse Zazi

CHOCOLATE ORANGE MOUSSE

The association of orange and chocolate is surely one of the greatest gastronomic affairs. The richness of chocolate and the zest of citrus do balance each other magnificently. This mousse is perfect for an intimate late-night supper, but is pretty good for ordinary dinner parties too. It's very simple to make and, despite the smoothness, has no cream in it. Do buy the bitterest chocolate you can – a lot of British 'dark' chocolate is very sweet compared to continental brands, so it's worth checking the chocolate for taste. Contains raw eggs.

INGREDIENTS
Serves 4

Juice and grated rind of 1 orange
115 g/4 oz dark bitter chocolate
4 tsp butter, preferably unsalted
4 large eggs, separated

Put the orange juice into a saucepan, break up the chocolate, add it to the pan and melt it gently over a very low heat, stirring regularly. When it's smooth, add the butter and grated orange rind. Let the butter melt and then beat the mixture till it's thick. Taking the pan off the heat, stir in the egg yolks and heat briefly until thick again. Be careful: too much heat gives you chocolate scrambled eggs. Leave to cool.

Beat the whites till stiff and fold the chocolate mixture into them. Pour into custard cups or wine glasses and chill for at least 2 hours. Especially nice with crisp, orange-flavoured biscuits.

MOUSSES 15

Chocolate orange mousse

CHOCOLATE TORTA

This Italian chocolate mousse is unusual in that it's baked.
This produces a very rich and firm mousse.

INGREDIENTS
Serves 4–6

225 g/8 oz dark bitter chocolate, with 70% cocoa solids
115 g/4 oz unsalted butter
4 eggs, separated
85 g/3 oz caster sugar
70 g/2½ oz plain flour

Break the chocolate up and put it and the butter in a non-stick saucepan over a very low heat. You may prefer to put them into a bowl and place that in turn in a pan of boiling water.

In a separate bowl, beat the egg yolks with the sugar and the flour. When the chocolate and butter are completely melted (do not let them boil!), add them to the egg yolk mixture and mix well together.
Beat the egg whites until stiff and fold in carefully.

Butter a 20-cm/8-in soufflé dish (you may wish to dust this with a little flour as well), pour in the chocolate mixture and bake at a very low temperature, 275°F/140°C/120°C Fan/Gas Mark 1, for approximately 45–50 minutes.
Take out of the oven and allow to cool out of the fridge for at least 2 hours. Chill for another 2 hours before serving. This is easiest served direct from the dish with a spoon, rather like moulding a firm ice-cream. It's very rich and is delicious served with thin lemon biscuits.

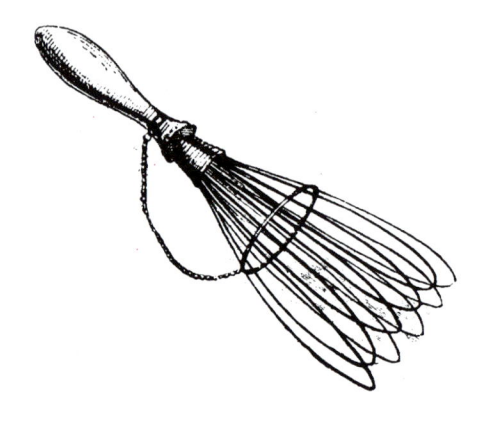

MOUSSES 17

Chocolate torta

CHOCOLATE AND HAZELNUT TART

This is an extraordinarily pretty pudding that only seems to last for about 30 seconds after you've put it on the table. Contains raw eggs.

INGREDIENTS

Serves 6–8

115 g/4 oz digestive biscuits
115 g/4 oz whole hazelnuts
75 g/3 oz butter, melted
55 g/2 oz light brown sugar
1 tsp ground cinnamon

FOR THE FILLING:

140 g/5 oz dark bitter chocolate
75 ml/2½ fl oz orange juice
7 g/¼ oz powdered gelatine
3 eggs, separated
225 g/8 oz mascarpone cheese, or any unsalted full-fat cream cheese
Whipped cream, whole toasted hazelnuts or grated dark chocolate, to decorate

Pre-heat the oven to 350°F/180°C/160°C Fan/Gas Mark 4.

Put the biscuits and hazelnuts into a food processor and blend until the mixture resembles fine breadcrumbs. Add the melted butter, sugar and cinnamon and mix thoroughly. Use to line the base and sides of a 25-cm/10-in loose-bottomed flan tin. Bake for 20 minutes, then remove from the oven and leave to cool.

Break the chocolate into small pieces and melt in a heat-proof bowl over a pan of hot water. Put the orange juice in a small heavy-based pan and add the gelatine. Stir thoroughly and heat very gently until the gelatine has completely dissolved. Remove from the heat and beat in the melted chocolate and egg yolks. Beat in the mascarpone cheese until the mixture is completely smooth.

Whisk the egg whites in a bowl until they are completely stiff. Fold into the chocolate mixture, using a large metal spoon, and spoon into the cooled biscuit case. Spread until the top is smooth and chill for at least 4 hours. You can decorate with whipped cream, whole toasted hazelnuts or grated bitter chocolate, if liked.

TARTS AND PUDDINGS

Chocolate and hazelnut tart

TORTA DI RICOTTA

There are a number of versions of this pastry-enclosed cheesecake made in the Neapolitan region of Italy. It's flavoured in a variety of ways too, with everything from *strega*, the yellow liqueur named after witches, through to the simpler and, to my taste, rather more pleasant flavours of citrus fruits. This calls for a substantial quantity of ricotta, the Italian equivalent of cottage cheese; British ricotta tends to be more liquid than the Italian version, and I follow Marcella Hazan, introducing a way of getting rid of some of the liquid in the ricotta before attempting to make the tart, which otherwise can come out a bit soggy.

I suggest you use shortcrust pastry for this. Very often, in Italy, they make a pastry that's extremely sweet, which I find overwhelms the pie. If you make your own shortcrust, you may care to add half a tablespoon of icing sugar to the mixture. If you're buying shortcrust, I'd just leave it at that.

INGREDIENTS

Serves 6

700 g /1 lb 9oz ricotta cheese
15 g/½ oz butter
115 g/4 oz chopped mixed peel
85 g/3 oz dark chocolate chips
2 tbsp caster sugar

Grated rind and ½ juice of 1 lemon
Grated rind and ½ juice of 1 orange
3 eggs, separated
450 g/1 lb shortcrust pastry (sweet if you can get it)

To prepare the ricotta, put it with the butter into a saucepan, preferably non-stick, and place over a medium heat, stirring gently from time to time. You'll find that it separates and quite a lot of liquid runs out. When you've cooked it for about 10–12 minutes, line a colander with a piece of muslin or, failing that, a piece of kitchen paper, and tip the mixture from the pan in, allowing the liquid to run away into a bowl or into the sink. Stir a little and leave in the colander until the mixture ceases to drip. Put the drained ricotta in a bowl, add the mixed peel, chocolate chips, sugar, the grated rind and ½ juices of the lemon and orange, and the egg yolks. Mix thoroughly and leave to stand.

Pre-heat the oven to $350°F/180°C/160°C$ Fan/Gas Mark 4.

Roll out two rounds of pastry, containing ⅔ and ⅓ of the pastry mixture. Grease a 20-cm/8-in spring-form cake tin (a loose-bottomed one will do too – you really do need easy ways of getting this out) and use the larger circle of pastry to line the tin, leaving a little proud at the top.

Whip the egg whites, mix these gently into the ricotta and fruit mixture, and use to fill the tin. Place the smaller pastry circle on top to make a lid and crimp the edges so that they stand up straight, rather like a small battlement around the pie.

Brush the top of the tart with a little beaten egg or milk, and bake for 45–50 minutes. The tart should be bright gold and the pastry cooked through but not dark brown. Remove from the oven and cool for 12 hours out of the fridge before serving.

TARTS AND PUDDINGS

Torta di ricotta

CHOCOLATE PYE

The recipe for this elegant English confection has appeared many times from my pen and kitchen. Each time it's slightly different as I change my mind about things. It is a recipe that has its origins in the eighteenth century and this version is easy to make, having lost nothing in the alterations I have made. You should serve only a small slice: it's very rich and moreish. Contains raw eggs.

INGREDIENTS *Serves 8*

FOR THE PASTRY:
140 g/5 oz butter, chilled
225 g/8 oz plain flour
Pinch of salt
55 g/2 oz sugar
1 egg yolk
3 tbsp water

FOR THE FILLING:
280 g/10 oz dark bitter chocolate
4 tbsp sherry or rum
1 tsp vanilla essence (for use with sherry)
1 tsp gelatine crystals
2 tbsp cold water
5 eggs, separated
Whipped cream, toasted almonds or walnuts, chocolate squares or flakes, to decorate

Pre-heat the oven to 375°F/190°C/170°C Fan/Gas Mark 5.

To make the pastry, rub the cubed chilled butter into the flour and salt, working lightly with your fingertips, until crumbs are reached. Fork in the sugar. Beat the egg yolk and water together, add and knead lightly. Leave the pastry to relax in a fridge for 30 minutes before rolling. You could of course make it in a processor or buy ready-made shortcrust pastry, as you choose. Either way, roll the pastry and use it to line a 25-cm/10-in tart tin, cover with greaseproof paper or foil and fill with dried beans. Bake 'blind' for 20 minutes. Allow to cool before filling.

Meanwhile, put the chocolate, broken into bits, in a round-bottomed bowl, and add the sherry or rum made up to 150 ml/¼ pint with cold water. (If sherry is used, add vanilla essence.) Set the bowl over a pan of boiling water and allow the chocolate to melt and get quite hot. Stir in the gelatine, softened in the 2 tbsp cold water, making sure it is totally dissolved in the chocolate mixture. Remove the bowl from the heat and beat in the egg yolks one by one. Leave to cool but not set.

Stiffly beat the whites and cut and fold these thoroughly into the chocolate mixture. Fill into the pastry case and put to set, but do not refrigerate (this would make the pastry go soggy). Decorate with a border of whipped cream, almonds or walnuts and chocolate squares or flakes. For high days and holidays, you might be able to lay your hands on some gold or silvered almonds, sugar rose petals or violets, which would make a truly opulent 'pye'.

TARTS AND PUDDINGS

Chocolate pye

CHOCOLATE AND CHESTNUT ROULADE

This all-time favourite dessert makes a sophisticated and festive end to a dinner party. Here I have suggested a chestnut cream filling, but once the technique of making a roulade has been mastered you could make all kinds of variations. Chopped fresh fruit, candied peel, chocolate shavings, all manner of flavourings can be added to the cream filling. Do buy good-quality chocolate, though, it makes all the difference. The roulade needs to cool in the tin for 8 hours after cooking, so this is best started the day before you plan to serve it.

INGREDIENTS

Serves 6–8

175 g/6 oz dark bitter chocolate, with at least 50% cocoa solids
2 tbsp water
5 eggs, separated
175 g/6 oz caster sugar
Icing sugar, to dust

FOR THE FILLING:

150 ml/¼ pint whipping cream
100–115g/3½–4 oz tinned chestnut purée
2 tsp caster sugar, or according to taste
Few drops of rum flavouring (optional)
2 candied chestnuts, chopped (optional)

Pre-heat the oven to 375°F/190°C/170°C Fan/Gas Mark 5.

Line the bottom and sides of a 32 x 23-cm/13 x 9-in Swiss-roll tin with baking-parchment. Melt the chocolate and water together over a gentle heat. Whisk the egg yolks and sugar together until thick, pale and mousse-like. Gently fold in the chocolate. With a clean, dry whisk, beat the egg whites until stiff, then fold into the chocolate mixture. Pour into the prepared tin and smooth to the edges. Bake for 15–20 minutes. The surface will have risen and have a crust. Gently press the centre to make sure it is cooked. Remove from the oven and cover with a sheet of baking-parchment and a tea towel, and leave to cool in the tin for at least 8 hours.

Uncover the roulade, laying the baking-parchment onto the tea towel, carefully invert the roulade onto this and peel away the lining paper. Trim the edges using a sharp knife. To make the filling, whip the cream until thick. Mash the chestnut purée together with the sugar and rum flavouring. Fold into the cream. Stir in the chopped candied chestnuts and taste for sweetness. Spread the roulade with the cream. Roll up lengthways, using the parchment to help you. (It is the nature of a roulade to crack.) Carefully lift onto a plate and dust with icing sugar. You can decorate with whipped cream, candied chestnuts or chocolate flakes, if you wish. This dessert can also be frozen quite successfully.

TARTS AND PUDDINGS 25

Chocolate and chestnut roulade

CHOCOLATE FONDUE

Ending a meal with a chocolate fondue is fun for everyone and goes down especially well with older children. It involves people dipping fruits of their choice into a communal pot of melted chocolate.

INGREDIENTS
Serves 4

115 g/4 oz dark bitter chocolate
55 g/2 oz mini marshmallows
A drop of milk
Selection of trimmed and peeled fruits cut into bite-sized pieces such as bananas, strawberries, kiwis, pineapple, peaches, apples, satsumas, pieces of cake or large marshmallows, to serve.

Melt the chocolate and mini marshmallows together in a bowl over a pan of hot water. (You may need to add a splash of milk to make the mixture smooth.) Mix well and you will have a thick glossy sauce.

Arrange the fruits, cake or marshmallows on platters and provide some skewers (forks will also work). Bring the chocolate bowl to the table and allow people to skewer the fruits and dip them into the sauce.

TARTS AND PUDDINGS

Chocolate fondue

TIRAMISU

Tiramisu was the fashionable pudding of the early '90s and uses mascarpone cheese, a full-fat Italian cheese, which is now widely available. However, full-fat cream cheese is a good alternative. Despite the north Italian provenance of mascarpone cheese, it's in Treviso that the dish is supposed to have first emerged. This is my own crafty version, as there are almost as many tiramisu recipes as there are cooks to prepare them. It makes a small attempt to control the calories by using some yoghurt. Contains raw eggs.

INGREDIENTS
Serves 4–6

2 eggs
250 g/9 oz mascarpone cheese, or full-fat cream cheese
140 g/5 oz Greek yoghurt
25 g/1 oz caster sugar
½ tsp vanilla essence
1 tbsp instant coffee granules
10 amaretti biscuits
55 g/2 oz dark bitter chocolate, grated

Separate the eggs and mix the yolks with the mascarpone cheese and yoghurt to a smooth paste in a large bowl. Beat in the sugar and vanilla essence until the whole mixture is smooth and glossy. Whisk the egg whites in a separate bowl until stiffened and fold into the mascarpone mixture.

Dissolve the coffee in three tablespoons of boiling water. Place the amaretti biscuits in a bowl and roughly break up. Sprinkle over the coffee and stir until well soaked. Put a layer of the soaked biscuits into a large glass serving-bowl or individual dishes, then spoon over a layer of the mascarpone mixture, put another layer of amaretti on top and finish with a layer of the mascarpone mixture. Sprinkle the grated chocolate on top to cover completely. Chill for at least an hour and up to six hours, and serve straight from the fridge.

TARTS AND PUDDINGS

Tiramisu

PEARS BELLE HELENE

This is a traditional French dessert – the combination of lightly poached pears, ice-cream and chocolate sauce is heavenly.

INGREDIENTS

Serves 4

4 large, firm, ripe pears
300 ml/½ pint water
55 g/2 oz sugar
225 g/8 oz vanilla ice-cream, the best you can find
Mint sprigs, to garnish

FOR THE CHOCOLATE SAUCE:

115 g/4 oz dark bitter chocolate, broken into pieces
55 g/2 oz butter

Peel the pears, cut them in half and take out the cores. Pour the water into a large saucepan and add the sugar and pears. Bring to the boil, then turn the heat down and poach the pears for about 10 minutes until tender, but not falling apart. Allow them to cool a little. Slice into a fan shape if you feel like it.

Make the chocolate sauce by melting the chocolate and butter together in a bowl over a pan of hot water. Be careful not to overheat the chocolate.

To serve, spoon the ice-cream onto 4 plates, pour a pool of hot chocolate sauce on each and lay 2 sliced pear halves on top of the sauce. Garnish with the mint and serve immediately.

TARTS AND PUDDINGS 31

Pears belle Hélène

HOT CHOCOLATE SOUFFLE

This is the most wonderfully rich pudding. It requires a moment or two's attention about 35 minutes before you are ready to eat it, but if you can sneak away from your guests or even your family, it's certainly worth the trouble. Do use the darkest bitterest chocolate available – you'll find it makes all the difference to the quality, texture and taste of the soufflé.

INGREDIENTS

Serves 4–6

100 g/3½ oz dark bitter chocolate
2 tbsp orange juice
4 egg yolks
70 g/2½ oz caster sugar
40 g/1½ oz plain flour
300 ml/½ pint milk
5 egg whites
Whipped cream, to serve (optional)

Pre-heat the oven to 400^0F/200^0C/180^0C Fan/Gas Mark 6.

Put the chocolate, broken up, into the orange juice in a small non-stick saucepan and place over the lowest possible heat, stirring until the chocolate has melted.

Whisk together the egg yolks and caster sugar, add the flour and pour in the melted chocolate, and beat well. Heat the milk in the saucepan which you used for the chocolate and pour into the chocolate mixture. Return to the pan and stir over the lowest heat until the mixture thickens like a custard. Leave it to cool.

When ready to cook, whip the egg whites until stiff but not grainy and fold them into the chocolate mixture very gently using a metal spoon. Pour into an 18-cm/ 7-in oiled soufflé dish and bake in the middle of a preheated oven for 30–35 minutes until fully risen. Serve immediately. People have been known to serve this soufflé with whipped cream. I wouldn't care to endorse it, for health reasons, but if you think you can get away with it – wow!

TARTS AND PUDDINGS

Hot chocolate soufflé

HOME-MADE CHOCOLATE ICE-CREAM

Home-made ice-cream often seems to be a matter of enormous complication – special machines or in and out the freezer and beatings and bashings. This is the simplest ice-cream I've ever discovered. Not only is it the simplest, it's also without question the most delicious. It's a style known in France as a *parfait* or, as we would say, perfect. Strangely enough I first discovered it in a Chinese take-away. It's foolproof, needs no special equipment, contains no crunchy bits of ice and tastes fabulous. Contains raw eggs.

INGREDIENTS

Serves 4–6

3 whole eggs
3 tbsp icing sugar
140 g/5 oz dark bitter chocolate
150 ml/¼ pint double cream
1 tsp vanilla essence

Whisk the eggs until they are lemon-coloured, frothy and thick. Whisk in the sugar, spoonful by spoonful, until it is all absorbed. Meanwhile melt the chocolate in a bowl over a pan of boiling water, then leave to cool.

In a separate bowl beat the cream until it is thick but not stiff. Add the vanilla to the egg mixture, and then fold in the cream gently, alternating with the chocolate, so you don't knock all the air out. Pour into a container and freeze for at least 4 hours. The ice-cream does not need stirring, but benefits from 30 minutes of softening in the refrigerator before serving.

TARTS AND PUDDINGS

Home-made chocolate ice-cream

PROFITEROLES

Perhaps one of the most widely enjoyed restaurant sweets in the world, profiteroles are really mini éclairs filled with whipped cream and with the chocolate coating still hot when they're eaten. They're a little trouble to prepare, but the choux pastry cases can be made ahead of time. They should only be filled an hour before serving. A great pudding to impress at a special dinner party.

INGREDIENTS
Serves 6

FOR THE CHOUX PASTRY:
250 ml/9 fl oz water (just under ½ pint)
55 g/2 oz butter
140 g/5 oz plain flour
4 eggs

FOR THE FILLING AND SAUCE:
140 g/5 oz double cream
55 g/2 oz caster sugar
115 g/4 oz dark bitter chocolate
55 g/2 oz butter
3 tbsp creamy milk
Grated rind of an orange

Pre-heat the oven to 425°F/220°C/200°C Fan/Gas Mark 7.

To make the choux pastry, bring the water to the boil in a small saucepan and add the butter. Add the flour in one go and stir continuously – it should form an instant paste. Stir and cook gently for 3 or 4 minutes. Take off the heat and add the eggs one at a time, beating the mixture well between each addition.

The pastry should now be pale golden and like sticky thick cream. Either take the choux pastry up in spoonfuls and place on a greased baking-tray, or better still, use an icing-bag with a 1-cm/½-in nozzle and pipe walnut-sized balls directly onto the tray. You should be able to make approximately 24. Either way, put the tray into the oven and leave to cook for 25 minutes. The buns will rise, so do make sure that you have left enough space between them.

When they're cooked and golden brown, take them out of the oven and prick a hole with a skewer or a knife at the top of each to let the steam escape and keep the shell crisp and firm. When they're cool, split each in half, and remove any soggy dough from the middle. Whip the cream and sugar together and use to fill the pastry, again a piping-bag is the easiest way. A dessertspoonful will go into each. Stack the profiteroles into a shallow pyramid, using a little of the cream as a kind of mortar, and put aside.

When you're ready to serve, melt the chocolate in the butter, add the milk and orange rind and stir until thoroughly mixed before quickly pouring it over the profiteroles. It is quite possibly one of the most fattening dishes in the entire world, and for its devotees, of whom I am one, well worth it.

TARTS AND PUDDINGS

Profiteroles

ADVANCED MARS® BAR SAUCE

It is an outrageous proposition to put this sauce over good-quality ice-cream, and it should only be done if you have no concern for calories. The sauce is, however, irresistible. I hardly feel able to recommend it but, as it's so easy and effortless to make, you might care to make up your own mind. Nevertheless, however good the sauce, the better the quality of ice-cream, the better the dish will taste. The availability of really excellent ice-creams, made from eggs and cream and fresh milk, is very encouraging.

INGREDIENTS   Serves 4
3 x 100 g/3½ oz or 4 x 65 g/2¼ oz Mars® bars
125 ml/4 fl oz milk
Ice-cream and chocolate flake bars, to serve

Cut the Mars® bars into 1-cm/½-in slices. Pour the milk into a non-stick saucepan, add the Mars® bar slices and heat gently, stirring until a thick caramel sauce is formed. (Do not let the mixture boil.) Pour over servings of ice-cream. Add a flake bar and serve immediately.

TARTS AND PUDDINGS

Advanced Mars® bar sauce

CHOCOLATE BISCUIT CAKE

A no-cook cake made very easily, and the favourite one of all with children. I know few adults who've turned it down either! As you can make it with the broken bits of biscuits left in the larder or the biscuit barrel, this can also be a very economical proposition indeed.

INGREDIENTS
SERVES 6–8

½ **orange**
225 g/8 oz sweet biscuits (I find ginger nuts and water biscuits, equally mixed, the best)
115 g/4 oz margarine
1 tbsp golden syrup
115 g/4 oz drinking chocolate
1 tbsp sultanas
1 tbsp raisins
55 g/2 oz chopped nuts (optional)

Put the orange, cut into quarters, peel and all, into a food processor and process until finely chopped, scraping down the sides if you need to. Add the biscuits and process until they are finely broken up like coarse breadcrumbs. If you do not have a food processor, then finely chop the orange and roughly crush the biscuits, you will end up with a more textured cake that is just as delicious.

Melt the margarine and syrup in a saucepan and beat until smooth. Beat in the drinking-chocolate powder off the heat, and add the sultanas, raisins and the chopped nuts, if you're using them. Pour the chocolate mixture into the processor and process it long enough to mix it all thoroughly (about 7 seconds).

Scrape it out and press into an oiled or non-stick 20-cm/8-in flan tin (lining it with oiled foil is a good idea). It will form a 2.5-cm/1-in cake which needs to be chilled in the fridge for at least 3 hours before eating.

CAKES AND BAKING 41

Chocolate biscuit cake

CHOCOLATE CHIP CAKE

This is always a favourite, combining the most scrumptious chocolate cake with the benefit of bits of chocolate buried within it. You can buy a variety of chocolate chips these days – my favourites are the dark bitter ones, but children often like milk chocolate better. Surprisingly, the chips don't disappear during the cooking but remain solid in the cake.

INGREDIENTS

Serves 6–8

175 g/6 oz plain flour
1 heaped tbsp cocoa
2 heaped tbsp drinking chocolate
1 tsp baking-powder
1 tsp bicarbonate of soda
115 g/4 oz caster sugar
2 eggs
150 ml/¼ pint milk
150 ml/5 fl oz vegetable oil, plus extra for greasing
115 g/4 oz chocolate chips
4 tbsp chocolate butter cream or apricot jam
Icing sugar, to decorate

Pre-heat the oven to $325°F/170°C/150°C$ Fan/Gas Mark 3/ or use the bottom of an Aga roasting oven.

Mix together the flour, cocoa, drinking chocolate, baking-powder, bicarbonate of soda and sugar. Whisk the eggs with the milk and vegetable oil, and beat that in turn into the flour mixture for 2–3 minutes with an electric mixer or wooden spoon until a smooth thick batter is obtained. Sprinkle two-thirds of the chocolate chips into the mixture, stir again and put into two 18-cm/7-in oiled and base-lined sandwich tins. Sprinkle the remaining chocolate chips on top of each cake. Make sure the surface of each is smooth and bake for 30–35 minutes until well risen. You can check to make sure they are cooked by pressing the top. If your finger mark springs back out then they're ready, if not they need another minute or two. Allow to cool a little, turn onto a cooling rack and cool completely.

Sandwich the cakes together with chocolate butter cream or apricot jam. You can ice this if you wish, or it's easily decorated with a little icing sugar sprinkled over the top.

CAKES AND BAKING 43

Chocolate chip cake

CHOCOLATE TRUFFLE GATEAU

Chocolate truffle gâteau is unashamedly rich, sumptuous and very special. This recipe is one I learnt from a great European *pâtissier*. Buy the best plain chocolate you can find.

INGREDIENTS

SERVES 10

140 g/5 oz dark bitter chocolate, with at least 50% cocoa solids
140 g/5 oz unsalted butter, softened, plus extra for greasing
150 g/5½ oz caster sugar
85 g/3 oz ground almonds
3 eggs, separated
100 g/3½ oz plain flour
Chocolate truffles or flakes, to decorate

FOR THE FILLING:

300 ml/½ pint double cream
200 g/7 oz dark bitter chocolate
55 g/2 oz raspberry jam

Pre-heat the oven to 350°F/180°C/160°C Fan/Gas Mark 4.

Melt the chocolate in a bowl over a pan of hot water. In another bowl, beat together the softened butter and 85 g/3 oz of the sugar until the mixture is fluffy, then fold in the melted chocolate, ground almonds and egg yolks.

Beat the egg whites and the rest of the sugar until white and forming peaks, then fold into the chocolate mixture. Sieve the flour on top and fold that in.
Pour into a greased 23-cm/9-in cake tin and bake for 40 minutes.
Remove from the oven and allow to cool.

While the cake is baking, make the chocolate cream filling. Bring the cream to the boil (you can do this quite safely with double cream) and add the chocolate, broken into small pieces. When the chocolate has melted, stir to a smooth cream and allow to cool for 1 hour.

Carefully slice the cooled sponge into three horizontal layers. Spread the middle and bottom layers generously with the jam and chocolate cream. Place the layers together and spread the rest of the chocolate cream over the top. Decorate with chocolate truffles or flakes, and if you have the will-power, allow to set.

CAKES AND BAKING 45

Chocolate truffle gâteau

CHOCOLATE BRANDY CAKE

A good simple cake for teatime, this is best eaten plain.

INGREDIENTS — SERVES 6

100 g/3½ oz dark bitter chocolate
1 tbsp brandy
3 large eggs
125 g/4½ oz caster sugar
25 g/1 oz cornflour
40 g/1½ oz self-raising flour

Pre-heat the oven to 375°F/190°C/170°C Fan/Gas Mark 5.
Melt the chocolate with the brandy in a small bowl over a pan of simmering water. Meanwhile whisk the eggs and sugar until pale and fluffy.

Sieve the two flours together and fold into the egg mixture. Pour in the melted chocolate, folding well in with a metal spoon. Pour the mixture into a buttered, base-lined 20-cm/8-in sandwich tin. Bake for 10–15 minutes.

'It's good. It's very rich. But my goodness it's moreish!'

CRAFTY CHOCOLATE CAKE

This is simply the ultimate chocolate cake – dark, moist, totally yummy and unbelievably easy to make. It is not totally wicked, as it is made with polyunsaturated oil, not saturated fats like butter. The method sounds deeply unlikely, but all I can say is, trust me! It is my family's favourite chocolate cake.

INGREDIENTS — SERVES 6–8

175 g/6 oz self-raising flour
1 heaped tsp baking-powder
4 heaped tbsp cocoa
115 g/4 oz caster sugar
150 ml/¼ pint milk
2 tsp black treacle
150 ml/5 fl oz sunflower oil
2 large eggs

FOR THE FILLING AND TOPPING:
350 ml/12 fl oz fromage frais
150 ml/¼ pint double cream
4 tbsp black cherry jam

Pre-heat the oven to 325°F/170°C/150°C Fan/Gas Mark 3.

Put all the cake ingredients into a food processor and blend together, or put them in a large bowl and mix with a wooden spoon, until the mixture is smooth, dark brown and creamy. Pour into two 18-cm/7-in greased and base-lined sandwich tins. Bake for 45 minutes then remove from the oven and take the cakes out of their tins. Allow to cool.

Beat the fromage frais with the double cream until thick and, when the cakes have cooled, spread one of them with cherry jam and a third of the cream mixture. Sandwich both cakes together carefully. Spread the remaining cream mixture on top and bring it up into peaks using a fork. You can refrigerate this for up to 24 hours before serving. Do make sure you use 18-cm/7-in sandwich tins – anything else could lead to either a biscuit or a gooey mess!

CAKES AND BAKING 47

Chocolate brandy cake (left) and Crafty chocolate cake

SUSIE'S AMERICAN CHOCOLATE CHIP COOKIES

If you have ever had those large, chewy, freshly baked warm chocolate chip cookies and wanted to make some yourself – this recipe is for you. These are the real McCoy!

INGREDIENTS
Makes 20–22 cookies

140 g/5 oz porridge oats
115 g/4 oz butter, softened
115 g/4 oz light brown soft sugar
115 g/4 oz muscovado sugar
2 medium eggs
1 tsp vanilla essence
225 g/8 oz plain flour
1 rounded tsp baking-powder
¼ tsp salt
55 g/2 oz dark bitter chocolate, grated
100 g/3½ oz dark chocolate chips

Pre-heat the oven to 375°F/190°C/170°C Fan/Gas Mark 5.

Blend the porridge oats in a processor until they resemble flour. Then tip out and set aside. If you do not have a food processor, buy the finest oats you can.

Cream together the butter and sugars, add the eggs and vanilla and blend. Add all the other ingredients, except the chocolate chips, and blend. Add the chocolate chips and pulse once or twice to blend, but try not to pulverise them. Form the dough into balls the size of a golf ball and place 5 cm/2 in apart on lightly greased baking-sheets. Bake for 10 minutes. Transfer to a wire rack to cool.

MOCHA BRIGADEIROS

Delicious sweetmeats to be eaten with a cup of coffee at the end of a meal.

INGREDIENTS
MAKES 24

397 g/14 oz can condensed milk
1 tbsp cocoa
75 ml/2½ fl oz strong coffee
1 tbsp butter
115 g/4 oz desiccated coconut

Put all the ingredients, except the coconut, into a non-stick pan and warm over a low heat until everything has melted and the mixture is smooth.
Pour into a greased bowl and allow to cool. When it is cold, wet your hands and shape the mixture into little balls. Roll the balls in desiccated coconut and chill for 1 hour before serving.

CAKES AND BAKING

Susie's American chocolate chip cookies

DYNAMITE BISCUITS

These biscuits will go down a treat with the kids on fireworks night.

INGREDIENTS   Makes 12

225 g/8 oz butter, softened
115 g/4 oz caster sugar, plus a little extra for dusting
225 g /8 oz plain flour
115 g /4 oz cornflour
115 g /4 oz milk chocolate
12 long pieces coconut shavings

Pre-heat the oven to 350°F/180°C/160°C Fan/Gas Mark 4/ or use the middle of an Aga roasting oven.

Place the butter, sugar, flour and cornflour in a food processor and blend until smooth and the mixture binds together. (You could do this by the traditional method, by creaming together the butter and sugar until soft and fluffy, adding the flour and stirring until the mixture binds together.)

Turn out onto a lightly floured board and knead gently until smooth. Press into a lightly buttered 20-cm/8-in square baking-tin. Prick well with a fork and bake for 45–50 minutes or until golden brown and cooked through. Leave for 5 minutes, then cut into twelve fingers and transfer to a wire rack to cool.

Meanwhile, break the chocolate into pieces and melt in a heatproof bowl over a pan of hot water. Dip one end of each biscuit into the chocolate and stick in a strand of coconut to make a 'fuse'. Place on a piece of non-stick parchment paper and leave to set completely, then transfer to an airtight container until ready to serve.

CAKES AND BAKING

Dynamite biscuits

FUDGE BROWNIES

Brownies are halfway between a pudding and confectionery. They are almost as gooey to cook as to eat, so non-stick baking-paper (widely available) is a good idea and saves quite dramatically on the washing-up. They are very tempting, but don't cut the squares too big; they're quite filling too. Unlike most cakes, they can be eaten hot, almost straight out of the oven, but brownies don't acquire their really tooth-sticking quality until they are cool.

INGREDIENTS
Makes 9

175 g/6 oz butter (or margarine)
55 g/2oz cocoa
175 g/6 oz soft brown sugar
2 eggs
55 g/2 oz self-raising flour
55 g/2 oz walnuts, chopped

Pre-heat the oven to 350°F/180°C/160°C Fan/Gas Mark 4.

Melt a third of the butter and add the cocoa. If you want to use a food processor for this recipe, put in all the ingredients, except for the walnuts, and zip for 5 seconds. If not, cream the rest of the butter with the sugar. Add the eggs and flour and then beat in the melted butter and cocoa mixture. Grease and base-line an 18-cm/7-in square tin. Stir the walnuts into the mixture, pour into the tin and smooth the top.

Bake for about 35 minutes. Leave for 5 minutes and then cut into squares. These can be eaten hot or cold and are often iced, usually before they're completely cool, with chocolate fudge icing.

Fudge brownies

CHOCOLATE TRUFFLES

Perfect with coffee after a dinner party – even when you have served mole poblano (see page 62) – truffles are sheer self-indulgence any time of the year, but particularly wonderful at Christmas. Make them the week before and hide them in the fridge – if you don't, they will instantly vanish!

They are better than anything you can buy, and cheaper to make.

INGREDIENTS

Makes approx. 400 g/14 oz

350 g/12 oz dark bitter chocolate
25 g/1 oz unsalted butter
25 g/1 oz ground almonds
3 egg yolks
2 tbsp double cream
Grated rind of 1 orange

POSSIBLE COATINGS:
About 2 tbsp cocoa, icing sugar, ground almonds or chocolate hundreds and thousands

Stir all the truffle ingredients in a saucepan and heat gently.
When the mixture has blended into a smooth consistency, remove from heat and pour onto a plate. Place in the fridge for an hour.

Sprinkle about 2 tablespoons of either cocoa, icing sugar, ground almonds or chocolate hundreds and thousands onto a Swiss-roll tin.
Remove the chocolate mixture from the fridge, scoop out a teaspoon at a time and form it into a ball. Then roll each ball thoroughly in one of the coatings.
Place the chocolates in paper casings and chill for at least 1 further hour.
Best eaten within 4 days.

CAKES AND BAKING

Chocolate truffles

DRINKS

CHOCOLATE MILKSHAKE

Whole milk may have its drawbacks for cholesterol-conscious adults, but it is important for children, particularly as milk contains so much essential calcium. This is a recipe unashamedly aimed as a treat for your offspring, though I am sure you will want to taste it first!

INGREDIENTS
Serves 2

1 tbsp drinking chocolate
2 tbsp boiling water
600 ml/1 pint whole milk
4 scoops chocolate ice-cream

Dilute the drinking chocolate with boiling water and stir until smooth. Pour the milk into a blender and add the chocolate paste. Spoon in the chocolate ice-cream and blend until smoothly mixed and foamy. Serve in tall glasses with a couple of straws.

REAL HOT CHOCOLATE

There is something almost naughty about a mug of real hot chocolate topped with Chantilly cream. But what better way to warm up after a brisk walk on a cold day?

INGREDIENTS
Makes 2 large mugs

55 g/2 oz dark bitter chocolate, with at least 50% cocoa solids
3 tbsp water
600 ml/1 pint milk
1 tbsp sweetened, vanilla-flavoured whipped cream (optional)
Ground cinnamon or cinnamon sticks (optional)
Marshmallows (optional)

Gently melt the chocolate in a pan with the water. In another pan heat the milk until scalding – do not let it boil. Pour the milk into the chocolate, whisking as you do so, to incorporate air and make the drink foamy. Pour into warmed mugs and serve. If you are feeling extravagant, top with sweetened whipped cream, flavoured with vanilla. You could also sprinkle the surface with ground cinnamon or use a cinnamon stick to stir the drink. A marshmallow floating on the top is a good treat. As an alternative, try mixing hot chocolate and strong black coffee to make a mocha chocolate drink.

PROPER COCOA

For those who prefer a less rich but equally chocolatey hot drink, there is nothing to beat a proper cup of cocoa.

INGREDIENTS
Makes 2 large mugs

2 tsp cocoa
600 ml/1 pint milk
Sugar, to taste

Put a teaspoon of cocoa into each mug. Add a splash of cold milk to each and stir until the cocoa is well blended. Heat the milk until scalding, then pour onto the cocoa, stirring all the time. Add sugar to taste.

DRINKS 57

Hot and cold chocolate drinks

HARE WITH CHOCOLATE SAUCE

This is a dish from Tuscany, where pappardelle, wide ribbon noodles (2.5 cm/1 in across) are served with a dark sauce made from mountain hare and flavoured with chocolate. If you can't make or find pappardelle, which are available in specialist Italian shops, tagliatelle work fine. The sauce is the thing. Although there's chocolate in it, you can't taste it as a sweet ingredient, more as a dark, rich background to the whole delicious exercise.

INGREDIENTS

Serves 4

900 g/2 lb hare, cut into pieces
55 g/2 oz plain flour
2 tbsp olive oil
1 large onion, chopped
4 cloves garlic, chopped
Salt and freshly ground black pepper
Juice of 2 lemons
225 ml/8 fl oz water
55 g/2 oz dark bitter chocolate
2 tsp dried oregano
Sugar, to taste
Buttered pappardelle or tagliatelle, to serve

Pre-heat the oven to 325°F/170°C/150°C Fan/Gas Mark 3.

Dredge the hare in the flour. Heat the oil in a pan and fry the hare until brown. Add the onion and garlic to the pan with the hare and fry gently for another 2–3 minutes. Season generously with salt and pepper and add the juice of the lemons, the water and the chocolate, broken into small pieces. Sprinkle over the oregano. Turn to make sure the ingredients are thoroughly mixed and put in the oven for 1½ hours.

At the end of the time, check the sauce for balance. It may need a little sugar if the chocolate was less than sweet. The flavour should be balanced between sweet and savoury, and the sauce dark and thick. Serve with plenty of buttered noodles.

SAVOURY SENSATIONS

Hare with chocolate sauce

BEEF WITH BALSAMIC VINEGAR AND CHOCOLATE

This is a tasty dark stew in which the chocolate blends into taste invisibility, although its presence is felt from the smoothness and richness of the sauce that bathes the chunks of meat.

INGREDIENTS   *Serves 4*

900 g/2 lb stewing beef
1 tbsp olive oil
1 tbsp butter
225 g/8 oz onion, finely chopped
2 cloves garlic, finely chopped
4 tbsp balsamic vinegar
400 g/14 oz tin chopped tomatoes
2 tbsp tomato purée
Salt and freshly ground black pepper
55 g/2 oz dark bitter chocolate
1 tsp dried thyme
1 tsp dried marjoram

Pre-heat the oven to 325°F/170°C/150°C Fan/Gas Mark 3.

Cut the beef into 4 cm/1½ in squares and fry gently in the oil and butter until browned. Add the onion and garlic to the meat and fry until translucent. Add the vinegar and boil briefly, scraping the sediment from the bottom of the pan. Then add the chopped tomatoes and tomato purée. Season well, add the chocolate, broken into small pieces, and the herbs, then add enough water to come just to the top of the meat.

Cook in the oven for 1½–2 hours until the meat is tender. A stir halfway through is of great benefit. This is delicious served with plain boiled rice and excellent with plenty of fluffy mashed potatoes. A green vegetable adds a good, sharp contrast.

Beef with balsamic vinegar and chocolate

MOLE POBLANO

Mole poblano is the great festive dish of Mexico and dates back to the time of the Aztecs, before the conquest of the country by Spain. Flavoured with all sorts of spices and with chocolate, this is very much a party dish, rich and very impressive. Classically it is made with turkey, but you can use chicken instead, simply adjust the quantities accordingly.

INGREDIENTS

SERVES 8–10

1 small turkey weighing 3–3.5 kg/7–8 lb, jointed into serving pieces
1 large onion
2 cloves garlic
2 red peppers
1 chilli pepper
2 slices white bread
4 tbsp cooking oil
400 g/14 oz tin chopped tomatoes
55 g/2 oz almonds
55 g/2 oz peanuts
55 g/2 oz sesame seeds
½ tsp ground allspice
½ tsp star anise
½ tsp ground coriander
55 g/2 oz dark bitter chocolate
Salt and freshly ground black pepper
Chopped fresh coriander or parsley
Toasted sesame seeds, to garnish

In a large saucepan, poach the turkey pieces in water until just tender. It will take about 45 minutes. While that is happening, peel and roughly chop the onion and peel the garlic. Trim, de-seed and roughly chop the peppers and chilli and roughly chop the bread.

When the turkey is just tender, strain off and keep the stock, pat the turkey pieces dry and fry them in the oil in a large pan into which they will all fit, until brown. Take out the turkey when it's brown on all sides, but keep the oil in the pan.

Put the onion, garlic, peppers, tomatoes and bread into a food processor and blend to a paste, then fry the paste in the oil in the pan. Put all the nuts, seeds and spices into the processor and whizz until finely chopped. Add this spice mixture to the tomato and pepper paste in the frying-pan and sauté for about 5 minutes.

Add 425 ml/¾ pint of the turkey stock and the chocolate, broken into small pieces. Check for seasoning. Bring the sauce to a gentle boil until the chocolate has melted. Stir thoroughly and add the turkey pieces, simmering them for about 25 minutes until thoroughly cooked. Put into a serving-bowl and sprinkle with chopped coriander or parsley and some more sesame seeds toasted in a dry pan. Serve with boiled, white rice.

SAVOURY SENSATIONS 63

Mole poblano

INDEX

Amaretti biscuits 10, 28
Aztec food 4, 62

Beef with balsamic vinegar and chocolate 60, *61*
Biscuits 48–51
    Dynamite 50, *51*
    Susie's American chocolate chip cookies 48
    Mocha brigadeiros 48, *49*
Brownies, Fudge 52, *53*

Cakes 40–7
    Chocolate biscuit 40, *41*
    Chocolate brandy 46, *47*
    Chocolate chip 42, *43*
    Crafty chocolate 46, *47*
Chocolate chips
    Chocolate chip cake 42, *43*
    Chocolate chip cookies, Susie's American 48, *49*
Chocolate, Real Hot 56
Cocoa
    bean 4
    powder 4, 42, 48, 52, 54, 56
    Proper 56
    solids 5

Drinking chocolate 4, 40, 42, 56
Drinks 56, *57*

Fondue, Chocolate 26, *27*
Fudge brownies 52, *53*

Gâteau, Chocolate truffle 44, *45*

Hare with chocolate sauce 58, *59*

Ice-cream 38, 56
    Home-made chocolate 34, *35*
Leaves, Chocolate 7

Mascarpone cheese 18, 28
Mars® bar sauce, Advanced 38, *39*
Melting chocolate 5–6
Milk chocolate 5, 42, 50
Milkshake, Chocolate 56
Mocha brigadeiros 48,
Mole poblano 62, *63*
Mousses 8–17
    Chocolate amaretti 10, *11*
    Chocolate orange 14, *15*
    Chocolate mousse surprise 8, *9*
    Chocolate mousse Zazi 12, *13*

Pappardelle 58
Pears belle Hélène 30, *31*
Profiteroles 36, *37*
Puddings 24–39
Pye, Chocolate 22, *23*

Ricotta, Torta di 20
Roulade, Chocolate and chestnut 24, *25*

Savoury dishes 7, 58–63
Soufflé, Hot chocolate 32, *33*

Tagliatelle 58
Tarts 18–23
    Chocolate and hazelnut 18, *19*
Tiramisu 28, *29*
Torta
    Chocolate 16, *17*
    di ricotta 20, *21*
Truffle gâteau, Chocolate 44, *45*
Truffles, Chocolate 54, *55*
Turkey 62

White chocolate 12

Numbers in italic type refer to illustrations